distorted thought in diluted wine

Aden McCracken

BookLeaf Publishing

India | USA | UK

Presentation by *BookLeaf Publishing*

Web: www.bookleafpub.com

E-mail: info@bookleafpub.com

ISBN: 978-93-5744-374-6

First edition 2022

In honor of the compassionate and loving life of Kristopher Yaniello. You will forever live within me and through me.

Onward and upward.

ode to grapes

originally published in
the Leland Quarterly

you are shriveled
like a raisin,
only meant to eaten
by the man who
is blind
to the wisdom that lives
deep in the canals of your skin
and deaf
to the soft notes that whisper
the sweet nothings of hesitation

he sinks his teeth
into you,
covering you
in his murky waters,
and his serrated fingers
cut into you
like the pages of a magazine
you are merely
a product
to be consumed,
and fault is easier to digest
when it's on you

so you don't say no

you can't
say no

Exit 48

A darkened mountainscape,
dotted with dim street lamps—yellowed
fallen stars, reaching out
to the above.
A highway, chasing
empty dreams, fogged by
the souls that drudge along its
edges. I'm starting to forget
why I'm holding on to
rusted guardrails.
When all I
want to do is throw
myself out the passenger side door and
into all that I've ever known.

silly boy

adapted from Halsey's "FUN GIRL"

i'm the silly boy

i'm the snort a line of Benadryl in front of my
friends boy
tell them it's just a joke even if it's just pretend
boy
the take a shot for every step i take boy
and never know when to take a break boy

i'm the tell you i can handle myself boy
even when i'd rather do anything else boy
the can't give myself a good look in the mirror
boy
vision goes out as i get nearer boy

i'm the gets off on getting taken advantage of
boy
will never know how to love boy
the spit in my face, pull out my hair boy
and tell you i like it, I swear, boy

i'm the wish i could take it back boy
pretend it didn't happen, but it's just a fact, boy
remember you were just a kid, boy
not like you could have hid, boy

so, when you can't smile all the time, boy
can't keep up with the rhymes, boy
can't be your silly self, boy
can't hold it together for everyone else, boy
remember you survived, boy
let yourself feel it inside, boy
it's okay that you want to get high, boy
and run away from the why, boy

but, sometimes
it's good to just cry, boy

toddler speak

every thought
sloshing in the pit of my stomach
coagulates as it reaches for
an escape at the surface
of my mouth.

black tar falls
down my lips,
splattering on my chest
in slurred tongue,
like a temper-tantrum-throwing toddler
spitting out SpaghettiOs
and crying out
in babbled voice

these shots
     of
poi–
        son
   dig
        a hole

in–
    "my head
    HURTS"

they won't

        "STOP LOOKING

           i'm

Fine

    i'm not

Weak

  what's Weak

about   trying

  to   find

a reason

   to–"

  STAY
  ALIVE

backstroke

you tread through waves. but, tread is an understatement. you are under. underwater that is, and you're going backward? liquid shelled bullets pierce through your nostrils and into your head. unconsciousness seems desirable to you now, yet instead you find yourself dressed in rusted metal. your skin is pruned, and like fruit, it peels, floating toward the surface, as if it's reaching out to the sun. from this distance, scars piece together constellations in a sky of warm undertones. you are prettier than you remember.

4:53 AM

escape the tomb, grab onto walls
bring nails to flesh, and feel it all

an ache to feed on poppy seed
before you even learn to feed

it lies beneath your yellowed skin
strawberry marked, and born from sin

you etch this name into your head
never forget the way it bled

painted a tale with foreign blood
a man and boy, not dad nor son

these dolls in hand, you play pretend
never began, can never end

in twisted tongue, you watch it turn
now let it sit, and let it burn

To the man who can't hear me:

Fabrics of intricate thread:
    Pinned against
    the window.
        Silent in the
        musty breeze.

A decapitated stuffed lion:
    Framed by
    three cigarette burns.
        Tossed against a wall where
        chipped paint meets stained
        carpet.

A crown of thorns:
    Embedded in
    the crown of my head.
        Bathing me in
        my own young blood.

I'm strapped to an old rocking chair.
I think it was my great-grandmother's, but
Thoughts are exchanges I can't afford, when
All I can feel are

Splinters of wood:
	Lodged into
	my calf.
		Keeping me silent
		to someone who I know isn't
		listening.

cutting edges with fingernail clippers

to drink
                    or
                              not to drink.

                    //

          to be happy
                    or
                              not to be

          anything.

                    //

          to feel
                    or
                              to forget
                    how to feel

          what it felt like
          before everything
          fell to ruin.

//

to cut each
finger off
       and

              sew them
           into your eyes

   so you don't
   have to see
the undoable damage.

What's already lost?

Blue and orange skies
kiss above a landscape
of dated mountains.

I'm merely
an avid onlooker,
longing to be in
a picture I thought
I had painted.

Lives move on
in front of me, and
like fluid
they dance
effortlessly
in a space where I'm
of no importance.

Yet, my eyes are glued
to the before,
to the what was,
to the what could have been.

anti-ode to bathroom stalls
stuck in my throat

it's funny how // blood paints // like red
watercolor it dilutes

and smears // color over my lips // smile painted
on

like a clown // i can hide hard feelings // but I
can't

let go of that *feeling* // when everyone
tells me // to do

nothing but sit down // shut up // and take a
shot // be funny // you are the funny
one. two. three. // more shots // make you
funnier

i guess // people don't like me
when i cry // when i'm not funny // when i'm
real and broken // twisted and mangled // hurt
and

just say nothing // sit down // shut up // and take
another shot // to the head would feel better

than faking it till // i can't make it // to a toilet
to empty my guts // and cleanse my sins //
anything that

comes out is a lie // and i'm lying
in vomit // and blood // but at least
i'm still masking // still lips
and stiller thoughts

lock and key

17

fighting gravity // it's not a simple task // when
your guts are spoiled

like rotten milk // you were left in a fridge //
light bulb

completely burnt out // burnt and branded
write on my entrance

little love poems // you spell out

a passcode // in your liquid // pushing past
conversation

between a pitcher and catcher // a whore and a
horrid

husk of corn // dry rub on the flesh
of an animal // who needs bred // swirling

your hips and tongue // spelling out //
S-H-U-T-U-P

T-A-K-E-I-T // like a real man or boy or slut or
whatever character in your script // sifting
through your head

like a VHS tape // sticky around my neck
your hands latch on // i'm riding a rollercoaster

at a park too familiar to feel // the rush
in my head // and to hear

the screams // locked
and keyed // in my throat

shower thoughts

are weird. it's five
a.m. and you
haven't slept since
yesterday

no the
day before
yesterday

yesterday was
a blur, but that doesn't
matter right now
what matters is–

fuck

turn the shower
handle to the
left–

shit
no

the right

that's right

left and
right really feel
the same when
your brain

is just as sunburnt
as your shoulders
and you
haven't slept since
yester–

god
you already
said that

today you
will say
the right things
maybe you'll
be serious
only serious
words and thoughts

are you serious?

no–shoot–yes
you are
sher-ious

sher-iously laughing
at the word sher-ious?

sh-o what,
and?

it's five a.m and
you're sher-iously hungover,
cackling about your
bubble pedo stache?

shower thoughts
are weird

20

you're
weird

21

Poem #13

is it strange?
am i strange?

strange thing to
say
think
feel
want
all i want
is to fuck everything

up

left   right

down

forward
backward

back in the depths
prancing around
with the

invisible monsters
that rip out my teeth
and eat them
in front of my face

a man with no face

why
are these
Jehovah's witnesses
  in
    my
      house,
staring at me
like i'm a
sinner–as if
the Barbie doll
in my hand
is a one-way ticket
to hell.

i know
boys aren't supposed
to play with dolls, but

      i.
don't.
    care.

i braid and
brush their hair.
i dress them and
give them

Names,
        Stories,
                and Lives–

where
boys who play
with dolls are
Loved
and not
in need of saving
from a man
with no face.

little lies

my dad used to tell me
that my name meant
little fire in Gaelic.

i always thought
he was lying:
silly little words
with no real
meaning.

but little did he know
his son
isn't his son,
and he is far from
just a
little fire.

he's
burning.

skin that is
no longer his chars.
kinders crack louder
than his insides scream
and beg to rip out
of their prison,
fall to the ground,
and flatten below
the feet of
passerby.

julembuary

it's been two years
since i first felt
pure #@^&$
course from
the tip of my tongue,
down into my
guts,
through my liver,
and into
the cluttered
cavern that is
[in fact]
my
fucked
up mind.

if God was real
he really
had me
on my knees
praying for Him
to give me a reason
to not
take the

cork off of
every bottle
i could find
and chug
them
like those
stupid
off-brand
fruit juice
barrels.

like
who the fuck
is Château d'Esclans
and why does
she
taste
like
rotten
piss
that–
          kinda tastes
          good?

she kisses me
like no one has before.

slobbery? yes.
spit reeking of piss? yes.

i ran
to my room,
held her in my arms,
and spun around
like the happiest
fool in the world.
i think i
dropped her,
       shattered her
       in pieces,
              and scattered her
              remains in the carpet.

but i didn't care
anymore
i didn't care
about anything
really?

A Day in DDA

feel it
slide between your teeth,
like flem
it's salty and sweet.
it's you,
but it's not you.
you are a foreign
invader
and the invaded.

look at
your skin.
you are a watermill.
red rivers
flow through your body,
carrying
faulty instructions.
you were built
to break.

remember
you are not
unique,
yet
unique
is all you've
ever known.

until now.

GROWING PAINS

an endless
stream of
water pours
through the spaces
between
my ribs,
holding me
together
like a velvet corset.

i am
a bathtub with
the faucet on and
drain unplugged

i can feel
my porcelain
edges sauter
to the tips
of my own fingers,
and
like iron i
am dense,
and i can't see
through

my own
irony

Undertow

Time is limitless sand
beneath us. *Limitless*.
It feels heavy in my mouth,
but I try to focus
on your salty breath–how crisp
it feels through
every inhale.

You reach out to
my fingertips, and tension
builds in my skin. But,
as I watch you
crash against the shoreline,
hang onto the edge
so effortlessly,
and embrace the
inevitable collapse–unfazed
by the turmoil you created
and the uncertainty that
lies ahead–I can't help
but be enthralled by you.

"I trust you."

You cradle me
in your intoxicating warmth,
letting me float
on your shoulders.

Your taste teases
the tip of my tongue
and fills my mouth.

I feel so light–so
Free.

You tell me that freedom
can only exist between us.

And when I try to swim
back to shore,
you pull me under.

War over falling petals?

I can feel my insides
destroying themselves like

I swallowed
>a whole
>Battleship board game
and forgot
>to read
>CHOKING HAZARD,
but I promise
>my eyes
>work.

I can see
>the red and white pegs
>pressing into my intestines
and I can read
>the instructions
>just fine.

HUNT!
HIT!
SINK!

WIN–
         a body
that is yellowing me
         from the inside
out and
         taking away
my will
         to keep going.

              I'm not a winner.

                    I'm
                       losing
                  a
                       game
                  I
                       didn't
              start.

         I wish I could
stop acting
         like I'm not struggling
to just live.

                         To breathe
                              and rest my
                    head at night is
                         a battle in itself.

      Ruminating
thoughts
         HAUNT me.
They don't

                              want me to
                                keep fighting.
                              They want
                                me to rot in

         their world,
but I don't want to live.
         Or die.
Or keep fighting.

         Or give up.

Evergreen

A fallen kingdom,
where hope no longer
lies; drowned out by
the dampness
of the wetlands and
shadowed by the mangroves;
loses its voice.

A sound so sweet–so
faint; and yet,
wielding the power
of a butterfly's flapping wings.

When looking to the guarding
walls, nestled in the heart of the
cobbled city,
you notice moss
bending around each stone,
filling in every opening.

And, as you listen closely,
focusing on intertwinement
and intersection; the unity
of fragmented and melded;
you hear the voice again.

It whispers to you,
Breathe underwater.